Tenpin Bowling Basics: Your Beginners Guide

ISBN-13: 978-1479118847

ISBN-10: 1479118842

Copyright Notice

TENPIN BOWLING BASICS: YOUR BEGINNERS GUIDE

Robert Hankley

I dedicate this book to every person – who has been lucky enough to have their lives touched by the joy, excitement and sheer buzz of tenpin bowling...

Contents

Tenpin Bowling:
A Brief History

The game which involves the act of knocking over a few pins with a ball isn't new, but it has remained as engaging and challenging as it was when people began playing it in the past.

There's a significant amount of evidence that point to bowling-type games having been played as far back as five thousand years ago.

Bowling is therefore among the world's oldest sports ever recorded, since it dates all the way back to the ancient Egyptian civilizations.

So, each time you put on those bowling shoes and head to your favourite bowling alley, you may take pride in participating in an old ritual and tradition people have enjoyed since about 3200BC.

About 90% of the game is derived from ancient Egyptian practices and the remaining 10% derived from law dodging in the 19th century.

When you add a splash of technology from the turn of the century, you'll have what's known as modern-day tenpin bowling.

According to historians, bowling hasn't changed that much from the time it was first developed until mid-19th century.

It was during this time that the ancient ninepin bowling game became very popular in Europe and soon found its way to the United States.

There, it became very popular with gamblers and was widely played by the underworld community.

As a result, the state government of Connecticut passed a law in 1841, which prohibited anyone from owning and operating a ninepin bowling alley.

This was the government's attempt at breaking up the gambling community by preventing them from meeting in bowling alleys, which was their usual gathering place. in an effort to get around the new law, the bowling alley operators simply changed the game's rules.

Instead of using nine pins, they started using ten and therefore transforming their businesses into tenpin bowling alleys.
These alleys were technically legal, since the Connecticut law only banned ninepin bowling.

And because tenpin bowling proved more interesting than its predecessor, more people preferred it and it's the game people play to this day.

When ten pins became the standard for bowling, the only aspect that remained old-fashioned was the bowling ball.

It was made of a variety of wood that's known as "lignum vitae" and it was valued for being both durable and lightweight.

The modern bowling ball was introduced only in 1905.

Perhaps the biggest difference between the ancient wooden bowling ball and bowling balls we use today is the fact that the wooden balls didn't have quite as much bounce or spring as the balls being used today.

This extra bounce is largely attributed to the rubberized material used in manufacturing the ball.

The very first rubber bowling ball introduced to the market in 1905 immediately became popular.

A new rubberized plastic compound was then created in 1914 for the specific purpose of being manufactured into bowling balls.

This new compound became known as Mineralite and the game of bowling was transformed by its arrival. It enabled greater precision along with significantly faster rolling speeds.

As a result, entirely new bowling styles and techniques were developed, many of which are still being used by the world's top bowlers today as well as by children who are just beginning to learn the sport.

Tenpin Bowling:
Popularity Reborn

A few years ago, the sport of tenpin bowling was immediately associated with either children's parties or middle-aged men.

These days, however, the sport is enjoying the rebirth of its popularity, as it is now considered the latest "cool" thing to do.

In fact, there are now more than 200 tenpin bowling centres across the United Kingdom and new retro bowling alleys are still being opened in London.

The British Tenpin Bowling Association is also seeing a burgeoning membership, which now exceeds 200,000.

Companies have begun entertaining their clients with what's known as "boutique bowling" during corporate functions. Even celebrities have been seen and photographed having a good time at the lanes.

According to the marketing manager of a bowling centre that has 25 locations across the United Kingdom, the sport started enjoying this renewed popularity when it was given a slight image change.

The owner of a retro bowling alley cum bar in central London says the design of his establishment was inspired by a Baltimore bowling alley, which gave him the idea that "cool bowling" has the potential for becoming popular.

One of the main reasons for this surge in popularity for bowling is said to be the fact that people have grown tired of the usual pastime of hopping around neon-lit bars.

Although some people don't really appreciate the new bowling shoes that are being offered for rent at bowling centres, many others are so enamoured by these shoes that one bowling centre manager has reported having more than 50 pairs stolen since the day they opened for business.

Furthermore, people are always asking if the bowling shirts and balls they have on display are for sale.

Because of this, a number of bowling centres have indeed gone into the business of selling bowling shirts as well.

Many of these places also feature a cocktail bar where customers can take a break after a round of bowling.

A number of experts say that bowling has become somewhat a "tired" sport a few years ago, which was why it needed to be rejuvenated.

And the new "cool" image was exactly what it needed to achieve such rejuvenation.

The idea for this new image stemmed from the growing popularity of themed pool bars, which was seen as a sign that people have grown tired of the usual drinking sessions and want to do more than just sink pints when they go out for a fun night out.

This is how the idea of putting up bowling centres with cocktail bars came into light.

In light of the changes and increased popularity of bowling as both a sport and a recreational activity, some bowlers and tournament organisers have remained sanguine.

These people are willing to accept any change as long as it helps the sport stay alive and draws the interest of more people to the game.

The game first saw its popularity fluctuate in the 1960s, and this continued through the 1980s, towards the end of which there were barely 50 bowling centres in the United Kingdom.

With its resurgence, new participants are welcomed by long-time bowlers in hopes that their enjoyment of the fun side of the sport will lead to the discovery of future league bowlers.

Tenpin Bowling:
Health Benefits

If you've ever watched movies or TV shows where tenpin bowling was featured, then you may have noticed that it's often portrayed as something that's not entirely healthy.

In any bowling scene on TV or the big screen, you probably see middle-aged overweight men smoking cigarettes and drinking beer in the middle of a bowling match.

Fortunately, Hollywood isn't always accurate in its portrayals.

The truth is that tenpin bowling does offer a number of health benefits and is, in fact, a legitimate sport. Otherwise, it wouldn't be included in the list of events for the 2012 Olympic Games, would it?

Among other things, tenpin bowling is said to have the characteristics of a weightlifting/tai chi combination.

Just think about it: The sport requires you to carry a ball that weighs anywhere between three and seven kilos, and then exert enough effort to propel this ball towards the other end of the lane to hit all ten pins.

This is the weightlifting part of bowling. The sport also requires you to have complete control over your body, as each movement you make needs to be calculated such that you're able to throw the ball properly. This is the part often compared to the discipline of tai chi.

Tenpin bowling is also a good calorie burner.

Just try playing a round of bowling and you'll be surprised at how tiring it can be as well as how much sweat you expend during the game.

Of course, it doesn't burn as many calories as a good workout, but burning 180-210 calories for each hour you bowl isn't that bad, is it?

If you choose to play three one-on-one games with a friend, it should take you about two hours to complete.

And statistics have shown that adding just 30 minutes to the first hour of bowling has the potential for doubling the amount of calories you burn.

As mentioned above, movies and TV shows have often presented bowling alleys as places where people indulge in such unhealthy habits as smoking and excessive drinking.

While most bowling centres these days may not allow smoking inside the premises, you could easily be tempted to drink beer with your buddies and eat junk foods while you bowl.

If you want to enjoy the health benefits of the game and avoid the unhealthy consequences, then you'd do well to drink water instead. And if you have to snack in between games, then you may as well bring some fruits or health bars with you.

In sum, tenpin bowling may not really be the best form of exercise.

However, if you regularly engage in the sport, then it can certainly help you gain a good amount of muscle tone and burn a good number of calories at the same time.

What's even better is that it successfully gets you off the couch and out of the house, where you probably don't feel like exercising much.

Becoming more active than you usually are is always a good thing, right?

So, what are you waiting for? Go out to the nearest bowling centre and start knocking those pins down!

Tenpin Bowling Rules

If you truly want to learn how to play tenpin bowling, then you need to know what the rules of the game are, of course.

Following is a quick look at these rules that should give you a good idea of how the game should be played.

Bowling Lane and Equipment

The playing surface in bowling is called a lane. It is typically 42 wide and 60 feet in length from the foul line to the head pin.

Each side of the bowling lane has gutters.

The area where a bowler plans and makes his move is called the approach. This area is 15 feet long and ends at the foul line.

The bowler is prohibited from stepping over the foul line in making his approach.

The pins are arranged in a total of four rows, with the head pin in the first row, two pins in the second row, three in the third, and four pins in the fourth and final row.

Each spot on which the pins are placed have specific numbers.

Take note that ordinary shoes aren't allowed in a bowling game because it can cause damage to the lanes.

First-timers are often surprised when they first realize that bowling shoes are deliberately unmatched.

Right-handed bowlers typically wear left shoes with relatively slippery soles and right shoes that have rubber soles to help them "brake."

Progress of Play and Scoring

A bowling game is comprised of ten frames, with each frame representing one turn for a bowler.

You're allowed to roll the ball twice in each turn. If you knock all ten pins down on the first roll, then you score a strike.

If you knock the pins down with two balls, then you score a spare. But, if there are still pins standing after the second roll is made, then it is called an open frame.

If you step over the foul line upon delivery, you commit a foul and any pin you knock down will be re-spotted, but the roll will still be counted as a shot. Pins knocked down by a ball that bounces off the rear cushion or the gutters aren't counted.

Take note that if you score two strikes on the tenth frame, you'll be awarded a final bonus ball. This means the highest number of strikes you can possibly score in a game is twelve.

Scoring twelve strikes is called a perfect game. If you score a spare in each of the ten frames of the game, you're said to have a clean sheet. A spare-strike-spare-strike performance throughout the game gives you a total score of exactly 200.

If you're able to reach an average of 200 or 210, then your skills will most probably be likened to that of a scratch golfer.

Your bowling average is calculated by adding up all of your scores and then dividing the figure with the number of games played. This is a good way of determining your progress in the sport. You may want to set a goal for increasing your average until you get to the same skill level as par bowlers.

How to Choose a Bowling Ball

If you're a recreational bowler, then you probably don't have a real need for worrying about which bowling ball to use.

After all, bowling centres naturally have them available at any given time.

However, if you're serious about learning how to compete in bowling, then one of the first things you need to know about the sport is that you need to choose a ball that can help improve your game.

Among other things, you'll have to determine the ideal weight, drilling pattern, and cover stock of a bowling ball that best suits your bowling style. Not only will the right ball help improve your scores, but also promote consistency.

Determining the Ideal Weight

Most bowling experts will tell you the ideal ball weight is about ten percent of your body weight, or up to 16 pounds.

This may be why most professional bowlers use 16-pound balls, although there are also many who use 15-pounders.

Another way to find the ideal ball weight is to add a pound or two to the weight of the usual house ball you bowl with.

Despite the added weight, the ball should seem to weigh the same as your house ball if it is drilled to fit your hand. Bear in mind that you should never use a ball that's too heavy just because you want to. It's important for you to be able to throw the ball comfortably.

Finding the Right Cover Stock

The cover stock is the material from which the outer surface of a bowling ball is made. Its value lies in determining the way a bowling ball will react to the conditions of the bowling lane.

There are generally four types of cover stock and they are polyester, reactive resin, urethane, and particle. Polyester is also often referred to as plastic.

This is the ideal cover stock for those who normally throw straight. Reactive resin and urethane are perfect for those who normally throw a hook.

Particle is ideal for experienced bowlers who already know how to react to various lane conditions and take control of the bowling ball.

Getting the Ball Drilled

While there are a lot of pre-drilled bowling balls available on the market, one that's drilled specifically to fit your hand allows you to control the ball better and significantly reduces your risk for getting injured.

If you're used to bowling with balls that don't fit your hand, then using the new ball that actually fits may seem awkward at first.

But, with enough practice, you'll realise the new ball is a lot more comfortable and controllable than any of the balls you previously bowled with.

There are stores that offer free drilling with ball purchase. But, even if drilling doesn't come for free, it should cost you no more than $30.

As soon as you've determined the right weight and cover stock you need in a bowling ball, you may start looking for a ball in online shops or at your local pro shop.

There are a few differences you should take note of depending on the category you're playing in, so you'll probably need to do a bit of online research or better yet, talk to the operator of your local pro shop to get some valuable advice.

Plastic balls are generally the least expensive balls, while particle balls are the most expensive.

The Need for Bowling Shoes

If you've watched professional bowling competitions at all, then you've most likely noticed that professional bowlers wear specially-designed bowling shoes on the lanes.

Why is this so?

What's makes these bowling shoes so different from your standard rubber shoes or sneakers?

Do they really make a difference in your game?

These are just some of the questions that may be going through your mind as you begin learning the sport.

And if you visit any bowling centre without proper bowling shoes, then you'll likely be asked to rent a pair. You need to understand that this isn't just a ploy being used by bowling centres to rip you off.

One of the most important parts of a bowling alley is the approach.

This is the particular part of the bowling lane on which you walk before you release the bowling ball to make a shot.

In order for you to achieve optimum performance, the approach has to be perfectly flat, free from any debris, and moderately slick.

This is the reason why bowling centres typically prohibit eating and drinking beyond a certain point. Just imagine how much of a hassle it would be to step on a piece of chewed gum just as you're walking up the approach to make your shot.

In the same way, bowling centres restrict the wearing of ordinary shoes on the bowling lanes to protect the approach and keep it in top condition.

If people were allowed to wear just any type of footwear on the bowling lanes, then there's a huge possibility of the approach getting filled with dust, dirt, and other debris scattered by people walking around.

Let's say, for example, the person who used the lane before you stepped on spilled soda on his way inside the bowling centre. As he bowled, his shoes may have left some sticky soda particles on the approach, thus giving you less-than-ideal playing conditions.

Naturally, bowling shoes help improve your performance in the game. But, beyond the performance benefits, they're strictly worn inside bowling centres for a number of important reasons.

Theoretically, these shoes are kept clean for the simple reason that people don't normally wear them outside bowling centres.

The condition of their soles, therefore, are far more controlled than if people were allowed to simply walk in from the streets and start walking around on the bowling lanes.

You may think bowling centres are trying to rip you off when they require you to rent bowling shoes, but they're actually just trying to keep their lanes in good condition.

Now that you're aware of the value of bowling shoes, you should remember not to use them outside, especially when it's raining or snowing.

In the same way, you should avoid wearing them inside bathrooms or even in the bar or lounge area of a bowling centre, where you just might step on spilled food or drinks.

Bear in mind that keeping the bowling lanes, and the approaches in particular, relatively clean and in good condition is important not only for purposes of having a good game, but for safety purposes as well.

When you're assured of your safety, then you'll be sure to have more fun.

Bowling Shoes:
A Buying Guide

If you're just starting to learn the sport of bowling and have never shopped for bowling shoes before, then you may not really know what to look for.

After all, you don't normally see people wearing bowling balls outside bowling centres, right?

Before you shop for a pair of bowling shoes, though, you may want to ask yourself if it isn't more advisable to just rent instead.

If you're taking up bowling simply as a hobby and you don't really expect to play that much, then renting is indeed the more practical option.

However, if you plan to compete in the near future and can see yourself bowling regularly, then it's definitely advisable to buy your own bowling shoes.

Performance or Athletic Shoes

When shopping for bowling shoes, you have the option of getting performance or athlctic shoes.

Performance bowling shoes, as the name suggests, are especially-designed shoes meant to help you achieve a better performance in the sport.

A pair of performance bowling shoes is typically comprised of one shoe for sliding and one shoe for braking.

On the other hand, athletic bowling shoes give you the look and feel of a standard pair of athletic shoes.

The difference, of course, is that they're made specifically for bowling. This type of bowling shoes is generally ideal for beginners as well as for people who bowl only once each week or less.

Professional Bowling Shoes and Their Soles

The sliding shoe of competitive or performance bowling shoes typically features a sole that allows the bowler to slide easily during his delivery.

In contrast, the braking shoe of performance bowling shoes features a sole that provides traction and is typically made of high-friction material such as rubber.

If becoming a competitive bowler is part of your plan, then you may want to consider buying a pair of bowling shoes with interchangeable sole pads.

This type of bowling shoes helps you ensure that your slide always matches the surface you bowl on as well as your bowling style.

Finding the Right Fit

Take note that there's a wide variety of widths for bowling shoes. Obviously, you wouldn't want to wear bowling shoes that are too tight. In the same way, it's also important to make sure your bowling shoes aren't too loose.

Remember that if your shoes don't fit snugly, you're likely to be thrown off your balance, which naturally has a negative effect on your game.

This makes it important for you to measure your feet or have them measured by a shoe professional. Even if you already know your standard shoe size, it's still better to make sure you get the exact feet measurements.

Other than those discussed above, it's also a good idea to bear in mind that shoes that feature collars, cushioned insoles and padded linings sufficiently provide you with added comfort.

Not only that, but these shoes also provide extra support and stability, as they minimise the movement of your feet inside the shoes.

This added support and stability, in turn, improves your balance, thus improving your performance as well. And if you want to achieve maximum comfort and "cool" with your bowling shoes, then you may want to look for a pair that features breathable uppers.

Tenpin Bowling Etiquette

So, you already know how to choose the right bowling ball. And you know there's a special type of shoes that need to be used for bowling.

Since you're serious about learning the sport, then you may already have gotten familiar with the game rules and scoring.

You may even have read up on the basic bowling techniques. You're raring to go to the nearest bowling centre to see how well you can put everything you've learned into practice. But, wait!

There's just one more thing you'd do well to learn before you start hitting those pins. You need to learn how to behave in a bowling centre.

Bowling is one of those sports where proper etiquette is essential so everyone can truly enjoy the experience.

Just like in fencing, it's common courtesy to follow a few guidelines when you go bowling.

The rules of bowling etiquette may have remained unwritten over the years, but that doesn't necessarily mean they're not being closely observed within bowling circles.

Here are some of the unwritten rules most commonly practiced by both recreational and professional bowlers worldwide:

1. General Bowling Etiquette

Always wear bowling shoes in the lane area to maintain the condition of the approach as well as other bowling equipment.

Be sure to remove your street shoes in the reception area, especially when they're wet, and keep them away from your bowling shoes so as to keep your bowling shoes clean.

In the same way, you should also refrain from bringing food and drinks to the lane area, as any spillage could damage the approach, thus making it dangerous for bowlers.

Finally, you should refrain from using nasty language or making loud outbursts, as these are generally considered disrespectful.

2. Dealing with Other Bowlers on the Same Lane

When it's your turn to make a shot, make sure you're ready.

It's considered impolite to make other bowler's wait as you get yourself ready.

You should also refrain from using another bowler's ball unless you've asked and was given permission to do so.

That's common courtesy, of course, not only in bowling.

Finally, you should be very careful not to step over the foul line. Not only is this against the game rules, but it could also have you tracking oil on the approach, which can be dangerous for you and for the other bowlers on that lane.

3. Dealing with Other Bowlers on Adjacent Lanes

If a bowler on your right is up for a shot at the same time you are, then common bowling etiquette dictates you should yield.

This means you need to step off the approach and out of the bowler's line of sight until he completes his turn.

You should also avoid intruding on adjacent lanes in any way and for whatever reason. This means you shouldn't throw your ball into the wrong lane, play or stand on the approach of another lane, or do anything that may be interpreted as infringing on the adjacent lane.

If you're serious about learning the sport, then you should seriously study and learn the above bowling etiquette by heart.

Bowling Styles and Grips

There are a number of bowling styles and it can be a bit difficult to identify which particular style a bowler adopts.

However, difficult as it may be, determining your style is important, as can help you identify the type of bowling ball you need to buy.

Furthermore, it can also help you understand what adjustments and improvements you may have to make in your bowling technique.

Here are the most common bowling styles:

1. **Stroker** – The stroker is identified by his smooth and precise delivery.

2. **Cranker** – A cranker typically uses a lot of wrist action so as to place a lot of power and a high number of revolutions into their shots.

3. **Power Stroker** – A power stroker has the advantage of a stroker's smooth release coupled with a cranker's power shots.

4. **Spinner** – A spinner is identified in the way he rotates the bowling ball on a vertical axis.

5. **Tweener** – A tweener is someone who has the ability to combine the different elements of stroking and cranking.

Other than the bowling styles, there's also a need for you to understand and learn the proper ways of gripping a bowling ball.

You can't just insert any of your fingers into those three holes and then launch the ball towards the direction of the pins.

Bowling is a game of precision, and there should be a technique to every single thing you do. A bowling grip can either be conventional or fingertip, and your bowling style or the kind of shot you plan to take largely determines which grip you use.

Conventional Grip

The conventional grip is common among beginners and recreational bowlers, primarily because house balls typically require this kind of grip.

This is where you insert your thumb all the way into one hole and then place your middle and ring fingers on the two other holes.

The good thing about this grip is that it allows you to hold the ball more securely, which is advantageous to a beginner, as it gives you more control of the ball.

The drawback, though, is that you may not be able to throw a hook quite as well as when you use the fingertip grip. It's a good thing you can easily switch from the conventional to the fingertip grip.

Fingertip Grip

The fingertip grip is used by most professional bowlers as well as many recreational bowlers with a real passion for the sport.

Similar to the conventional grip, you also need to insert your thumb all the way into the thumb hole and then your middle and ring fingers into the inserts.

The difference, which you'll surely notice immediately, is that the thumb hole will seem too far away with a fingertip grip.

The advantage of this grip is that it allows for easier release and better rotation.

It also provides you with an increased lift and more ball control. It's definitely a good idea to master this grip if you want to become an excellent bowler.

Tenpin Bowling
Adjustments

One of the major factors that play a huge role in improving consistency in bowling is you ability to adjust to lane conditions.

The moment you step onto a lane, you have to know what adjustments you need to make, how to make them, and when you should make these particular adjustments.

In fact, one of the most common and significant mistakes committed by novice bowlers is the refusal to adjust accordingly.

Sure, you may be able to score a strike on your first row, but that doesn't necessarily mean you can consistently bowl strikes for the rest of the game without making any adjustments. If you want to get high scores consistently, you definitely need to learn how to read lane conditions and then adapt accordingly.

In this section you will learn more about the different bowling adjustments as well as when and how to make them.

1. Lateral Adjustments

This adjustment involves changing your starting position either to the left or to the right.

This is necessary for when you're missing the left or the right pockets while delivering relatively good throws.

Remember not to change your target and your approach in this case. All you need to change is your starting point, depending on which pocket you're missing.

2. Forward/Backward Adjustments

If you're not very comfortable with making a lateral adjustment, then you may try to move backward or forward instead.

If you're a right-handed bowler missing the right pocket, then you need to move back a bit on the approach. If you're missing the left pocket, then you need to move forward. All you need is to step back or forward one step to make this adjustment.

3. Finger Position Adjustments

A common mistake bowlers make is taking their index and pinky fingers for granted. You need to realise that adjusting the positioning of these fingers allow you to put more or less hook on the ball.

For less hook, you need to spread your fingers wider. For more hook, you need to bring your fingers closer together.

When you've mastered the art of making these subtle changes, you may want to make a finger position adjustment in each of your shots.

4. Speed Adjustments

It's a good idea to make speed adjustments if a lateral adjustment doesn't solve your initial problem of missing the pockets. As a general rule, more speed results in less hook and less speed results in more hook.

If your ball keeps hooking to the wrong side, then you may want to add some speed. If the ball fails to hook at all, then it's a good idea to lessen the speed.

5. Ball Adjustments

There are times when you still keep missing the pocket even when you've already made lateral, forward/backward, finger position, and speed adjustments.

This is the perfect time to consider changing balls. If the ball keeps failing to hook, then you may want to find a ball especially-designed for heavy oil.

This adjustment is often used only as a last resort primarily because changing balls too often leaves you unsure of which ones work and which don't.

How to Throw a Hook

If you want to graduate from being a novice bowler to at least a serious recreational bowler, then you definitely need to learn how to hook a bowling ball.

Bowling requires precision in order to achieve success and throwing a mean hook is one of the ways for you to attain precision.

1. Get the Right Ball

You may already have a good technique, but if the ball you're using fails to catch friction on the lanes, you won't be able to successfully execute a hook.

As a general rule, balls made from reactive resin or particles are ideal for throwing a hook on practically any lane, with the exception only of extremely dry lanes.

And when you've found the right ball, you also need to make sure it's drilled properly, depending on your personal bowling style.

Although this isn't really a requirement for throwing a hook, it can make the task a lot easier for you.

2. Use the Right Grip

By now, you're probably already familiar with both the conventional and the fingertip grip.

As a beginner, though, it's highly likely that you've been bowling almost exclusively with the conventional grip, where your middle and ring fingers are inserted into the hole up to the second knuckle.

If you take the time to closely observe professional bowlers, though, you'll realise most of them use the fingertip grip, where the middle and ring fingers are inserted only up to the first knuckle.

This grip makes it easier to hook the ball, since it provides you with more revolutions as well as more control over the ball.

3. Learn the Swing

Although you may use as many or as few steps as you want when making the approach, a four-step approach is generally recommended for throwing a hook.

Right-handed bowlers would do well to step forward with their right foot first and vice versa for left-handed players.

Push off the ball as you take your first step and then swing your arm such that the ball is held parallel to your ankle on your second step as you start bending your knees. As you take your third step, the ball should be held at the top of your backswing.

Swing your arm forward and then release the ball as you finish with a slide. Don't forget to follow through with your arm even as the ball is released.

4. Make Adjustments as Needed

Once you become comfortable with the swing and release, you should be able to execute it consistently and adjust your footwork accordingly.

Be sure not to force the swing in any way and make the necessary adjustments based on lane conditions as well.

Remember that as you play in more advanced games and more challenging lanes, it may not be enough to make lateral adjustments.

You may have to make a few speed and finger positioning adjustments as well. As long as you're able to read the lane conditions and game situation accurately, it should be easy for you to properly adjust your play.

Finding Your Strike Ball

Like any other bowler in the world, you probably want to get a strike on every single shot you throw.

But, of course, that is much easier said than done. Getting a strike on every throw requires consistency, which is why you need to find you "strike ball."

This is the type of shot you can consistently throw and achieve good results with. This will then serve as the basis for any adjustment you make and for improving your game overall. And the first thing to do in order to find your strike ball is to choose a starting position.

If you're a right-handed bowler, then you may start by lining up your left foot with the centre dot on the approach and then placing your right foot in the most comfortable position, depending on your bowling style.

The next step is to choose your target. Ideally, this should be the second arrow from the right of the lane.

Aim to have your ball roll directly over this arrow as it approaches the pins.

You may not realise it, but most of the oil on a majority of house oil patterns is in the middle of the lane.

Therefore, having your ball land on the outside assures you of more traction down the whole length of the lane.

Observe what happens to your shot. If the throw resulted in a perfect strike, then try to replicate it on every throw. If you miss in any way, then make the necessary adjustment.

If you somehow fail to hit the pocket consistently from your initial starting position, then you need to move towards the direction of your miss.

For example, if you keep missing left, then try moving a few boards to your left when you make the approach.

Do the opposite if you keep missing right. Regardless of the direction of your adjustment, though, be sure to aim for the same arrow on the lane.

Take note that it may take just a few throws or even a number of games for you to find your strike ball.

As a general rule, the more balls you throw, the more you'll get a feel for how your shot reacts to the lanes. More practice will also make you more aware of what you need to do in order to achieve consistency.

Of course, strictly speaking, there's no rule in bowling that says you have to aim at the second arrow all the time. If you decide to throw a huge hook, for example, then you may want to consider aiming at the first arrow.

On the other hand, if you're still having problems throwing a hook, then it may be a good idea to aim more towards the middle of the lane.

Another simple adjustment you can make in an effort to find your strike ball involves speed.

Throwing the ball slower gets more hook on it and throwing it faster lessens the hook. All of these other adjustments, however, are best done once you've found the ideal starting position.

You'll be glad to know these adjustments are likely to come naturally as you start getting a better feel for throwing the ball.

Picking Up Spares

As you learn the sport of bowling, you'll naturally want to score strikes all the time.

Realistically, though, that isn't likely to happen. This is why you also need to learn how to pick up spares, as this is an essential part of attaining high scores in bowling.

If you've been observing other bowlers do their thing, then you've most likely noticed some advanced bowlers using plastic balls to pick up spares.

However, that's not really necessary. In fact, there are a lot of talented bowlers who successfully pick up spares using only one ball.

Naturally, you want to get a strike on your very first shot – and every shot thereafter – but, that may not always happen. In the event you fail to throw a strike, you'll naturally have to make an adjustment so you can pick up a spare. The necessary adjustment is actually simple math.

In most cases, you simply need to adjust your starting position. That means you throw the ball with the same speed you used on the first throw and aim at the same target.

Check the pins and make sure you know exactly which ones are left standing before applying the advice below.

Depending on what pins are left standing, you need to move four boards either to the left or right. Your decision should be based largely on where the remaining pins are positioned on the lane.

Let's say, for example, you moved four boards to the left of you initial starting position and then aimed at the same target using the same speed, the ball is likely to hit the pin deck four boards to the right of your first shot.

Of course, this isn't an exact science, since other factors such as the way the oil is laid out or the manner in which it's breaking down will affect the ball. But, it's a good place to start if you truly want to hone your bowling skills as you go along.

What do you do if the pin left standing is the one, two, five, or nine pin?

The best thing to do in this case is to aim from the same starting position.

If the ball left standing is either the three or the six pin, then it's best for you to move four boards to the left to let the ball hook earlier.

If you happen to leave the four or eight pin standing, then you need to move four boards to the right so the ball will hook later. If it's the ten pin that's left standing, then you need to move eight boards to your left so the ball will hook right into the pin.

Finally, if it's the seven pin that's left standing, then you need to move eight boards to the right.

Now, what if you leave more than a single pin standing?

In that case, it's best to use your common sense.

For example, if the one and three pins are left standing, then you should know that you can simply aim for the one pin and deflect it to hit the three or perhaps move two boards to the left in order to hit both pins at the same time.

While the above guidelines give you a general idea of how to pick up spares, you'll have to use your experience and common sense in most cases.

Tenpin Bowling Myths

Myths often have a semblance of truth and the same is true of the most common bowling myths.

There are instances, however, when people believe certain things and accept them as absolute truths even when they're really not.

Here are some of the most common bowling myths, along with an explanation of what the truth behind them really is:

Myth #1: The Ability to Throw a Hook Makes You a Great Bowler

All professional and top amateur bowlers throw a hook almost with every single shot. This has led to the common belief that bowlers who throw a hook are automatically better than bowlers who don't.

While the ability to throw a hook does increase your chances of scoring a strike, what actually makes an excellent bowler is the ability to control the hook rather than just to throw one.

Myth #2: Hitting the Head Pin Guarantees a Strike

Many people believe – and would even advise you accordingly – that the only thing you need to do in order to guarantee a strike is to hit the head pin.

If you've ever gone bowling even once in your life, then you know this isn't necessarily true.

Generally speaking, it's true that you need to hit the head pin in order to bowl a strike. However, simply hitting the head pin doesn't necessarily guarantee that all the other pins will follow. The secret is in hitting the head pin correctly.

Myth #3: You Need to Use a 16-pound Ball at All Times

In all levels of competitive bowling, the maximum weight allowed for bowling balls is 16 pounds. This has led many people to believe that you need to use a 16-pound ball at all times in order to play a good game.

Remember, though, that regardless of the ball's weight, you need to be able to throw it properly in order to play a good game. This means a 16-pound ball isn't really advisable if it's too heavy for you.

After all, how can you expect to get those strikes if you can hardly swing the ball properly in the first place?

Myth #4: Bowling a Good Game Means You Can Go Pro

Once you've experienced scoring a perfect game, you may immediately think it's easy enough to go pro. This is what commonly happens to novice bowlers.

They watch professional bowling competitions and notice the top professional bowlers score an average of 220-250 for every competition. So when they score a perfect game twice in a row, they automatically think going pro isn't all that difficult.

Bear in mind that it takes more than just a good game or two to truly play like a pro. Professional bowling isn't just about accuracy; it's about consistency as well.

Myth #5: You Can Buy a Good Game

Just like in many other sports, some people tend to think one can bowl better simply by buying the latest and most expensive bowling equipment.

There may be some truth to this, as new shoes can indeed offer better traction and a new ball reacts more to the lanes.

More than new equipment, though, you need to make sure you have the right equipment that fits your bowling style to make sure you always bowl a good game.

Top Reasons for Joining a Bowling League

League bowling is currently among the most popular recreational sports and if you aren't already a league bowler, then chances are good that you know at least one, even if you're not aware of that person being a league bowler.

Since its inception, league bowling has given several hours of enjoyment and challenge to a lot of people, and it still continues to do so. The good news is that there are leagues for all types of bowlers.

Whether you're one of the best bowlers in your locality or you don't really care about winning and are simply playing to have fun, there's surely a league for you.

There are even couples leagues available, if you want to enjoy the sport with your significant other. Here are some of the best reasons for you to join a bowling league:

1. Fun and Relaxation

Bowling is a lot of fun. There's no question about that.

Joining a league makes it more so, since it gives you the opportunity to bowl with like-minded individuals at least once each week.

Bowling also gives you a welcome respite from a hectic work week. This is especially true if you're taking up the sport simply as a hobby and you don't really get too stressed when you're score isn't that high.

You could simply show up, throw a few shots to unwind and give your muscles a good stretch, and enjoy the company of other league members.

2. Camaraderie

The word "camaraderie" is most often thrown around in team sports such as hockey. But, it isn't exclusive to team sports.

Bowling also often allows you to develop camaraderie with other league members, especially if you regularly bowl with family members and friends.

Some of the regulars who started out as strangers may even become your friends for life simply because you spend a few hours each week throwing a few frames together.

You'll be surprised at how many people actually join bowling leagues just so they can banter with others while playing the game they love.

3. Fitness

Many people aren't aware – and probably wouldn't believe – that bowling actually offers some health and fitness benefits. Well, it's not exactly the equivalent of a good workout, but it can definitely help you maintain your fitness gains from working out.

And if bowling is the only bit of exercise you get each week, then you'll be glad to know it helps you burn a considerable amount of calories. Of course, you can't expect it to lead you towards having a well-sculpted physique.

But, surely you can understand how the act of repeatedly hurling a heavy sphere towards a specific target can help develop muscular endurance and strength.

4. Money

Most bowling leagues don't have any objection to small-time gambling. In fact, half of the league fees often go towards the actual bowling while the other half goes towards a prize fund.

At the end of each season, you and the rest of the team will receive prize money depending on where you finish. In most cases, there may also be individual prizes up for grabs.

Other than that, there are additional ways of earning a pittance when you participate in league bowling.

These include strike pots and card games.

Printed in Great Britain
by Amazon.co.uk, Ltd.,
Marston Gate.